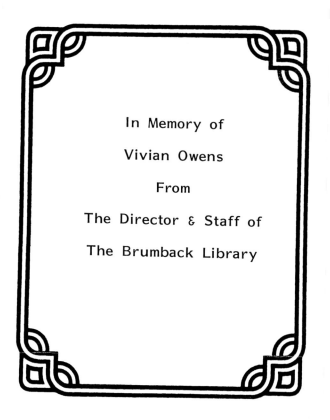

In Memory of

Vivian Owens

From

The Director & Staff of

The Brumback Library

TOOLS FOR TEACHERS

- **ATOS:** 0.8
- **GRL:** D
- **LEXILE:** 200L

- **CURRICULUM CONNECTIONS:** animals
- **WORD COUNT:** 71

Skills to Teach

- **HIGH-FREQUENCY WORDS:** a, be, for, from, in, is, it, that, the, then, what
- **CONTENT WORDS:** beak, bugs, chick, chicken, egg, feathers, head, scratches
- **PUNCTUATION:** periods, exclamation points, question mark
- **WORD STUDY:** r-controlled vowels (*chirp*, *dirt*, *feathers*); short /e/, spelled ea (*feathers*, *head*); /ng/ (*coming*, *hungry*); short /u/, spelled o (*coming*)
- **TEXT TYPE:** factual recount

Before Reading Activities

- Read the title and give a simple statement of the main idea.
- Have students "walk" though the book and talk about what they see in the pictures.
- Introduce new vocabulary by having students predict the first letter and locate the word in the text.
- Discuss any unfamiliar concepts that are in the text.

After Reading Activities

Encourage children to talk about the different things chicks are shown doing in the book. List the different behaviors, such as hatching, scratching, and resting, on the board and consider which farm babies (piglets, foals, calves, etc.) might do the same things. Would a calf scratch for bugs? Would it rest? Following the children's suggestions, write the animal's name underneath the behavior and discuss the appropriateness of each match.

Tadpole Books are published by Jump!, 5357 Penn Avenue South, Minneapolis, MN 55419, www.jumplibrary.com

Copyright ©2018 Jump. International copyright reserved in all countries. No part of this book may be reproduced in any form without written permission from the publisher.

Editor: Jenny Fretland VanVoorst **Designer:** Anna Peterson

Photo Credits: Getty: Sungjin Kim, 10–11. Shutterstock: Africa Studio, cover; Szasz-Fabian Jozsef, 1, 12–13; Pjjaruwan, 2–3; saied shahin kiya, 4–5; Anneka, 6–7; Tsekhmister, 8–9; lyly, 14–15; Oleksiy Avtomonov, 16tl; schankz, 16tm; DSBfoto, 16br.

Library of Congress Cataloging-in-Publication Data
Names: Mayerling, Tim.
Title: Chicks / by Tim Mayerling.
Description: Minneapolis, Minnesota: Jump!, Inc., 2017. | Series: Farm babies | Audience: Age 3–6. | Includes index.
Identifiers: LCCN 2017008829 (print) | LCCN 2017009935 (ebook) | ISBN 9781620317655 (hardcover: alk. paper) | ISBN 9781620317853 (pbk.) | ISBN 9781624966125 (ebook)
Subjects: LCSH: Chicks—Juvenile literature. | Chicks—Pictorial works—Juvenile literature. | Chickens—Juvenile literature. | Chickens—Pictorial works—Juvenile literature.
Classification: LCC SF498.4 .M39 2017 (print) | LCC SF498.4 (ebook) | DDC 636.5—dc23
LC record available at https://lccn.loc.gov/2017008829

CHICKS

by Tim Mayerling

TABLE OF CONTENTS

tadpole
books

Chirp! Chirp! What is that sound?

egg

It is coming from the egg!

The egg wobbles.
Then it cracks.

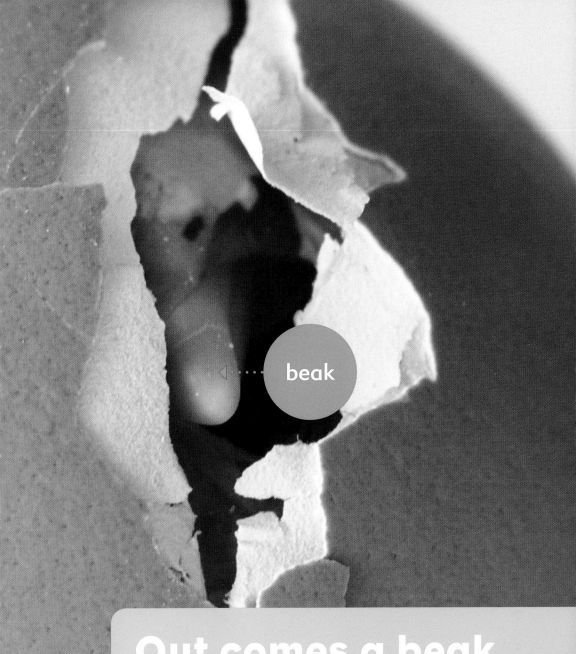

beak

Out comes a beak.

Then comes a head.

It is a chick!

It stands. It fluffs its feathers.

Soon it is dry.

The chick is hungry.
It scratches in the dirt.

It looks for bugs.

The chick will eat.

Then it will rest.

It will grow.